THE 100
GREATEST
DAD JOKES
OF ALL TIME

1st Edition, 2020
Innovate Publishing
www.innovatepublishing.ca

ISBN (eBook): 978-1-7774451-0-2
ISBN (Paperback): 978-1-7774451-6-4

"There is nothing in the world so irresistibly contagious as laughter and good humour."

~ Charles Dickens

How do you weigh a millennial?

In Instagrams.

Why does Snoop Dogg always carry an umbrella?

Fo' Drizzle.

I invented a
new word today:

Plagiarism

Did you hear about the French cheese factory that exploded?

Da brie was everywhere!

Growing up, my mom always said I could be anyone I wanted to be.

Long story short, identity theft is a crime.

I was going to tell you a time-travel joke, but you didn't like it.

Why can't you hear
a psychiatrist use
the bathroom?

Because the 'p'
is silent.

What do you call
a fat psychic?

A four-chin teller.

My wife asked me
to stop singing
"*Wonderwall*".

I said maybe.

What does a buffalo say before he leaves for work?

Bi-son.

What's the difference
between a hippo
and a Zippo?

A hippo is really heavy,
and a Zippo is
a little lighter.

How do you organise
a space party?

You planet.

What's the fastest liquid on earth?

Milk - because it's pasteurized before you even see it.

Why are skeletons
so calm?

Because nothing gets
under their skin.

How many tickles does it take to make an octopus laugh?

Ten-tickles.

What do you call an illegally parked frog?

Toad.

Dad Advice:

Never open emails about canned meat. It's spam.

What did the grape say when it was crushed?

Nothing - it just let out a little wine.

Why are spiders
so smart?

Because they find
everything on the web.

Did you hear about the circus fire?

It was in tents!

I had a joke to
tell you about
1-ply toilet paper.

But it's tearable.

Did you hear that new song that costs only 45 cents?

It's 50 Cent featuring Nickelback

My wife says
that I *never* listen -
which is a funny way to
start a conversation if
you ask me.

Rick Astley will let you borrow any DVD from his Pixar collection.

But he's never gonna give you *Up!*

Dad Advice:

Never buy anything with velcro.

It's a total rip-off.

Fun Fact:

Dogs can't operate MRI machines.

But catscan.

What do Alexander the Great and Winnie the Pooh have in common?

They both have the same middle name.

What do vegetarian
zombies eat?

GRRAAAIIINNNSSS!

I used to really
hate facial hair,
but then it grew on me.

Fun Fact:

6:30 is the best time of day, hands down.

Why do cows have hooves instead of feet?

Because they lactose.

Why is Peter Pan always flying?

Because he Neverlands.

Why do bees have sticky hair?

Because they use a honeycomb.

What's the best way to watch a fly fishing tournament?

Live stream.

How many ears does Spock have?

Three - the left ear, the right ear, and the final front-ear.

I invented a pencil with two erasers.

But it was pointless.

I'm reading a horror book in braille.

Something bad is going to happen. I can feel it.

I think I might take up meditation.

I figured, hey, it's better than sitting around doing nothing.

What do you call an elephant that doesn't matter?

Irrelephant.

What did the janitor
say when he jumped
out of the closet?

"Supplies!"

I was just reminiscing about a beautiful herb garden I had growing up.

Good thymes, good thymes.

Did you hear about the guy who invented *Lifesavers*?

He made a mint!

Did you see the *Yelp!* review for the first restaurant on the moon?

"Great food, no atmosphere."

What do you call two octopuses that look the same?

Itenticle.

What size clothing
do psychics wear?

A medium.

To the person who stole my antidepressants,

I hope you're happy now.

I used to work at
a juice factory,
but got fired.

Apparently,
I couldn't concentrate.

Why did the invisible man turn down the job offer?

He just couldn't see himself doing it.

What do Santa's elves listen to while they work?

Wrap music.

Fun Fact:

The guy who invented the knock-knock joke won a 'No-bell' prize.

RIP Boiled Water:

You will be mist.

Do you know what my grandfather said to me before he kicked the bucket?

"Hey! Watch how far I can kick this bucket!"

Dad Advice:

Never tell a 'dad joke'
if you're not a dad.

That would be
a faux pa.

What did the drummer call his twin daughters?

Anna One, Anna Two.

Why did the scarecrow win an award?

Because he was out-standing in his field.

I'm reading a book about anti-gravity.

It is *impossible* to put down!

Why do skeletons never go trick or treating?

Because they have no-body to go with.

To the person
who stole my
Microsoft Office,

I will find you.

You have my Word.

I thought about going on an all-almond diet.

But that's just nuts.

Fun Fact:

Sometimes I tuck my knees into my chest and lean forward.

That's just how I roll.

I told your mom
she drew her
eyebrows too high.

She seemed surprised.

Dad Advice:

Never trust atoms.

They make up everything.

I saw a robbery at the *Apple* store today.

So technically I'm an iWitness.

Fun Fact:

Seven out of four people are bad with fractions.

I'm working on a new
song about a tortilla.

Well actually,
it's more of a wrap.

There are two goldfish in a tank.

One goldfish says to the other, *"I'm gonna be honest, I have NO idea how to drive this thing."*

To the person who
stole my glasses,

I will find you.
I have contacts.

Fun Fact:

If a child refuses to nap, they're technically resisting a rest.

What do you call a
small donkey
with three legs?

A little wonkey.

I asked Siri for the time and it said, *"7:53am. And don't call me Shirley."*

I'd accidentally left it in *Airplane!* mode.

I know a lot of jokes about retired people.

But none of them work.

I think my wife has been putting superglue on my antique weapon collection.

She denies it, but I'm sticking to my guns.

Thought of the Day:

If two vegans
get in a fight,
is it still considered
a beef?

A Vicks VapoRub truck spilled its entire load across the freeway.

There was no congestion for 8-10 hours.

Fun Fact:

Diarrhea is hereditary.
It runs in your jeans.

What time did the
Dad go to the dentist?

Tooth hurt-y.

What do you call
26 letters that
went for a swim?

Alphawetical

How do you reheat cold Hawaiian pizza?

On aloha temperature.

"Dad, did you get a haircut?"

"No, I got them ALL cut."

A ham roll
walks into a bar
and asks for a drink.

The bartender says,
*"Sorry, we don't
serve food here."*

Your mom said, "*What rhymes with orange?*"

And I told her, "*No it doesn't!*"

Why do chicken coops only have two doors?

Because if they had four, they'd be chicken sedans.

Why don't eggs
tell jokes?

Because they'd crack
each other up.

Dad Advice:

Never trust stairs.

They're always up to something.

Did you hear the
rumour about
the butter?

Well, I'm not going
to spread it.

Did you hear about the man who fell into the upholstery machine?

He's okay.
He's fully recovered.

Why couldn't the bicycle stand up by itself?

It was two tired.

"Dad, can you put my shoes on?"

"No, I don't think they'll fit me."

Why can't a nose be 12-inches long?

Because then it would be a foot.

How do you find Will Smith in the snow?

You just follow the fresh prints.

I don't want to brag, but I just finished a puzzle in 6 weeks!

On the box it said 1-2 years.

What do you call
cheese that isn't yours?

Nacho cheese!

How does a penguin
build a house?

Igloos it together.

I bought the world's worst thesaurus yesterday.

Not only is it terrible, but it's *terrible*!

What did the left butt cheek say to the right butt cheek?

"You crack me up!"

I just invented the corduroy pillow.

It's making headlines!

Why can't melons get married?

Because they cantaloupe.

What do you call it when Batman leaves church early?

Christian Bale.

Do you know why elevator jokes are so good?

Because they work on so many levels.

I have the *best* joke about nepotism.

But I can only tell it to my kids.

What's Forrest Gump's email password?

1forrest1

FROM THE AUTHOR

Thanks for reading *The 100 Greatest Dad Jokes of All Time.*

I hope you, your friends, and your family got some big laughs from it.

As a small business and self-employed writer, my Amazon review rating means everything for my success and continued growth.

If you can spare a few moments to leave a positive Amazon review it would go a long way towards helping others decide about my books.

Thank you and I look forward to seeing you again in the next book!

CHECK OUT OUR OTHER TITLES:

THE 100 FUNNIEST KIDS JOKES OF ALL TIME

THE 100 GREATEST KIDS RIDDLES OF ALL TIME

THE 100 GREATEST KNOCK KNOCK JOKES OF ALL TIME

THE 100 GREATEST PARENTING JOKES OF ALL TIME

100 *MORE* OF THE GREATEST DAD JOKES OF ALL TIME

Printed in Great Britain
by Amazon

72664766R00061